HOW TO START AND RUN AN AFTER SCHOOL DRAMA CLASS

THAT KIDS (AND PARENTS) WILL LOVE!

Life's like a play: it's not the length,
but the excellence of the acting that matters.
- Seneca

Running a drama program is easy and fun and your students will remember the experience for a very long time. It's great to be able to give the gift of acting to a child, because I know they will use it throughout their entire lives.

Curt Jackson
RecreationPros.com

How to Start and Run an After School Drama Class
That Kids and Parents Will Love / by Curt Jackson

Cover Design: Curt Jackson
Cover Graphic: © Hemul I Dreamstime.com
Editing: Sandy Goodson

ISBN-13: 978-0615433998
ISBN-10: 0615433995

To contact author, email curt@recreationpros.com

Table of Contents

INTRODUCTION

Like most kids I caught the acting bug in elementary school. School plays were always so much fun. I loved playing one of the main supporting roles, being the guy behind the guy. I was never interested in being a lead. There was too much pressure.

All during school I was one of those class clown types. I loved being the center of attention. However, it was a little different "performing" in front of an audience of people I didn't know. That was scary. Never the less, I loved acting and wanted to be an actor when I grew up.

One sunny day during recess, the school music/drama teacher took me aside and asked me to be a lead in the sixth grade musical. I was in the fifth grade.

With fear in my throat and a hint of flattery in my eyes I asked her if I would have to sing a solo. She told me that I would, as though she expected me to be excited about it.

I declined. It wasn't that I couldn't sing, it was that I didn't want to be judged by sixth graders and their parents. Kids can be ruthless if you're not in their "circle". I was scared to death.

After constant prodding from the drama teacher I finally agreed, despite my fear and reservations.

The first practice was a nightmare. I felt the eyes of all the sixth graders, only a couple of whom I knew by name, burning into my back. I just could not muster up the courage to sing in front of the other students with any projection whatsoever.

After a few rehearsals it was evident that I was not going to be the star the teacher had hoped for.

My solo became a duet.

On the night of the performance my nerves got the best of me. It wasn't just my singing the audience could hardly hear but my dialogue as well.

I was mortified. I told myself I would never act or sing again.

When I was 13 I was involved with a local youth group. The teen coordinator decided to start a drama team.

As there were only six teenagers that were interested in being a part of the team the coordinator strongly encouraged me to participate.

My stomach started turning, remembering the awful experience I had endured just a few years prior. I shared my feelings with the coordinator and we talked about how important it was for me to "get back on the horse".

I'm thankful to this day for his encouragement and understanding.

He was serious about making sure the drama team was prepared. He brought in a few acting coaches to help us improve on our skills.

As I went through the exercises with everyone else I gave it my all. I really went for it and put myself out there. It was a lot easier since I knew everyone there and felt comfortable around them.

After the final day of training one of the acting coaches took me aside and said that he was impressed with me and that I should think about pursuing acting for real. I was speechless. Chills ran down my back. Woo Hoo! Somebody thinks I'm good.

Looking back on it, the acting coach was probably just a local drama teacher, but his words were sunshine to my soul.

This is the power that teachers, coaches and mentors have.

For the next two years our little drama team traveled all over California performing for youth groups, in public venues and for large camp groups. We performed a variety show with sketches and songs, and people of all ages loved it.

After that I moved around a lot and got involved with sports. I continued taking acting classes through school and other organizations.

Having grown up an hour from Hollywood, I was always interested in giving acting a shot as a career. I continued to take acting classes, but there was always a reason why I couldn't dedicate the time to pursue my acting dream; school, work, relationships, fear of rejection, etc.

Instead of choosing acting as a career I chose recreation. I have never regretted the decision.

My first recreation job was as a camp counselor at a resident (sleep-away) camp. For those of you who have been to a resident camp you probably remember those good old campfires.

The first night of each week was a campfire put on by the staff. We would teach the kids camp songs and entertain them with skits. The campers would roar with laughter, even though many of them knew the skits from the year before.

Throughout the week counselors would work with their campers to prepare them for the ending campfire. That's when the campers would get the chance to perform.

I always enjoyed working with my cabin groups, teaching them how to enter the stage and working with them on their lines. Campfires were my favorite part of camp.

After years of working in the camp industry I was excited to use the "variety show" model in after school drama classes. I won't lie, I was a bit nervous about how it would go over with the kids and their parents.

Thankfully, everyone who has been involved with my classes has been extremely pleased.

This book is a resource for youth leaders and teachers that lead after school classes and programs. It assumes no dramatic experience or training of your students. Even youth leaders that have very little drama experience can run a successful program using this book.

This program is geared towards 3 – 9 graders,

Here you'll find pages full of information and easy action steps, including games and activities designed to teach and entertain, that will help you get your drama program up and running.

I know you will find this book to be an indispensible resource.

Good luck with your program and I hope that you empower many kids to rise up and act.

- Curt "Moose" Jackson

Please Note:

In this book I use the words class and program interchangeably. While the word "class" can be used to describe a one time educational session it can also used to describe a series of classes. A program can mean a one time event, a series of classes, or a collection of different classes.

The same goes for the words skits and sketches. I usually refer to the short 3-5 minute plays as sketches in the book, but in the Resources area they are refered to as skits.

One more thing - the book goes over how to start and run an 8-10 week series of one hour, once-per-week classes. However, you can just as easily run a 12 week program as noted in chapter 3.

1

THE OPENING ACT

THE NUTS AND BOLTS OF SETTING UP A DRAMA PROGRAM

Congratulations on taking the first step towards starting an after school drama program.

Before getting started with the details of setting up a drama program I want to introduce you to the model I use, the variety show drama program.

Let's first go over the two most popular types of drama programs and then compare them to the model I use...

TYPES OF DRAMA PROGRAMS

THE PLAY

When an organization decides to put on a play, it's a big deal. It's a lot of hard work, but it can be very exciting and rewarding.

The last school I worked at had 150 students try out for the play. I certainly never had 150 kids register for my programs…thank goodness. There is only one of me and I would have to turn away a lot of kids.

With a play production you need to:

- hold auditions
- gather parent volunteers
- get sets made
- fit costumes
- raise funds
- rehearse
- pull your hair out
- schedule the stage area for rehearsals and performances
- market the play so you fill the seats
- work with the actors 2-3 times per week
- pull more hair out
- bite your nails
- organize the lights and sound
- set up VIP seating

…you see where I'm going with this? More power to the school play directors that do this year in and year out, but I'll leave it to them.

Unfortunately, only a few students get the lead roles and only a few more actually get speaking parts. The others merely fill the supporting, non-speaking roles; the elves, Oompa-Loompas, trees, etc. Also, the actors get very little instruction on acting.

Play directors do not have time to teach the actors how to act. She or he expects them to pretty much know how to do that already.

THE DRAMA CLASS

The youth drama class is all about teaching the art of acting.

It's an hour+ class for 8-10 weeks full of games and instruction. This is not a bad way to go.

There is no need to deal with any of the details listed above; the sets, volunteers, auditions, etc. In fact most kids really enjoy acting classes and you'll be able to run a drama class using this manual.

With a little more preparation and work though, you can set it up so that your "class" has an end game. This would be the variety show that you put on at the end of your 8, 10 or 12 week session.

THE VARIETY SHOW DRAMA PROGRAM

While I use Saturday Night Live to help describe to parents and students what my drama program is all about, there are no bands, sets, opening monologue or cameras in our final performance.

Instead, each 1 hour and 30 minute class is divided into two parts. The first half of the class is filled with games and instruction to help each student become better actors. The second half of the class is for sketch rehearsal.

"It's Saturday Night!"

Sometimes parents or board members don't quite grasp the concept of a variety show. I use Saturday Night Live to help describe to them what my drama program is all about. While there are no bands, elaborate sets, opening monologues or cameras in our final performance, there are 8-10 comedy sketches that have nothing to do with one another.

The Variety Show Drama Program vs. The Play

- No costumes are needed (some simple costume items that kids can throw on over their clothes is always nice to have though).
- No sets are needed.
- No props are needed (again some simple hand held props are always fun).
- An army of volunteers is unnecessary (I run the program by myself or with the help of one other staff member).
- Sketch dialogue is easier to learn and memorize then the multitude

of lines needed for a play.

- (Most Importantly) Each child gets the chance to have a lead role. In a play there are a limited number of lead roles. With 6-8 sketches, each child has the opportunity to be the star.

The Variety Show Drama Program vs. The Drama Class

- The kids get to act in a final performance for their friends and families.
- Parents love that their children are performing.
- The kids get to put into practice all the lessons they learned from the instructive classes.
- It's down right fun, and makes my heart feel good to see them perform.

I hope you are on board with running a variety show-type program.

If a simple drama class is what works for your situation, then I won't try to convince you otherwise. In a simple drama class the first 5 weeks or so students should learn about acting and play plenty of drama games. During the last few weeks they can rehearse and perform the sketches in front of each other for fun.

Are you ready to get started? Let's do it...

BEFORE YOU BEGIN

There are a few things you should do before the program even starts. As with anything, the more prepared you are once things get rolling the better.

NAME THE PROGRAM

Are you the type of person that likes to be creative when naming programs and classes? I hope so.

A good name gives programs some pizzazz. It makes it stand out.

Kids and their parents would rather sign up for Curtain Call All Stars: A Youth Drama Program as opposed to a class called The Basics of Drama.

Here are some suggestions:

> Curtain Call All Stars
> Young Actors Studio
> Exit Stage Right
> Encore!
> The Young (your city) Players
> The Goof Troupe: An Acting Class with a Lot of Fun and Laughter
> On Stage: A Introduction to Youth Drama
> Lets Act!

PLAN YOUR DATES

I know planning the dates seems like an obvious thing to do, but I want to stress how important it is to plan the class dates and the performance date.

Imagine that there are only 2 or 3 weeks left of class.

You have finally decided on a date for the performance.

You do not want to send out notices of the performance to the parents only to find out that the parents did not have enough time to plan for it and are now going to miss their child's performance because of a prior engagement.

Worse yet, you do not want to find out that one of your students cannot make it.

Since this is an after school program and most of the parents are working after school, the performance will need to be held in the evening.

So plan the date and time in advanced.

SCHEDULE THE STAGE

Whether you are using the local school's stage or a community center stage you will most certainly need to book the date well ahead.

If your community is anything like the ones I have worked for the stages and auditoriums are constantly in use. Sometimes it can be very difficult to nail down a date to use the stage.

Take care of this as soon as you know when you want to hold your performance.

GET THE WORD OUT

Marketing is always something that needs to be done, especially for a new class.

If you work for a recreation department, YMCA, etc. and you have a brochure that goes out to all the parents in your community then that is a good start. Most recreation leaders, specialists or coordinators will stop at that, and sometimes that is all that will be necessary to fill a class.

If you want to do some extra marketing and make sure the class will get enough students then worry not. In Chapter 6 I have given you 20 ways to market your drama program. Many of the ideas can be used to market other classes as well.

CREATE NOTEBOOKS

During the second week, when you introduce the sketches to the students, give them a three ring binder with all the scripts, along with a few pages of key acting tips.

Purchase the binders that allow you to slip a piece of paper into the cover of the binder. Create a page with the name of your class, a neat graphic or two and the student's name.

PLAN THE CLASSES

Plan the class out in advance.

You should already know what you are going to teach, what games you plan to play and what sketches you will rehearse.

 It's always a good to have more games ready then you think you'll time for.

It's not uncommon to finish a class ahead of time. You scratch your head and wonder, "How did that happen?" The kids stare at you in jeopardy of being bored. You can either have them rehearse their lines or you can reach into your "bag of tricks" and play a new or favorite drama game.

You'll find lesson plans in Chapter 3 that will give you an idea of how to run the classes.

A SAMPLE CALENDAR
based on a 10 week program

Many weeks before (depends on when your brochure/advertising comes out)

- Book the stage on a date that is during the final week of your class or the week after the class ends.
- Set the dates of the classes. You'll probably need to do this to get it in your next brochure or catalog.

Two weeks before the first class:

- Purchase your notebook binders.
- Create the cover page for the binders
- Add your scripts and acting tips to the binders.

One week before the first class:

- Read over the lesson plan for the first class
- Call the parents and ask them for their email address if you don't already have them. (You'll learn why a little later.)

While you have them on the phone, or leaving a message, tell them how excited you are that their daughter or son is going to be in the class and ensure them that they will have a great time and learn a lot.

Parents love the personal touch of hearing from the instructor. In fact, I suggest you do this for all the classes and programs you run. It takes a little extra time, but is well worth it.

- Make a list of props and clothing you might want to use for the sketches. This way you can ask the kids later on if they have any of these items at home.

By not having to purchase these items you are able to keep your costs low.

- Order shirts.

I love handing out shirts for all my programs. Its great marketing for future programs and the kids love it.

The shirts may cost you $10-$15 each, but you can tack the cost on to the registration fee.

The shirts should have the name of the program, the program logo if there is one (You may want to use some form of the happy and sad drama masks or a curtain), the name of your organization and its logo.

 Black is a very dramatic color for shirts. For the younger kids purple seems to be very popular.

There are three ways to handle sizes of t-shirts:

- Ask for a shirt size during registration (this is what I prefer).

- Wait until the first class to get the sizes of all the students.

- Order enough shirts for 3 seasons or more.

This will allow you to get a better price on the shirts. You will also be able to surprise the students since they had no idea they were getting a shirt.

If you go with this option make sure you do not have a date printed anywhere on the shirt (i.e. Exit Stage Left - Drama Program 2009). On the next page you'll see an example.

ACTION PLAN

The following action plan should be used to make sure that you haven't forgotten anything as you put together your new drama program.

- ☐ Give your program a name – be creative and fun.
- ☐ Decide on the dates of the classes.
- ☐ Decide on the date of your performance.
- ☐ Schedule the use of the stage or area you will be using for the performance.
- ☐ Create a marketing plan and market your program.
- ☐ Create your student notebooks.
- ☐ Plan out each class. You can use the lesson plans from Chapter 3.

2

CAN'T WE JUST PLAY SPORTS?

10 REASONS YOU SHOULD BE RUNNING A DRAMA PROGRAM

Most youth recreation organizations have a wide array of sports classes and for good reason. Sports are very popular with all ages. They are very good for kids physically and mentally.

While sports programs are very popular, they aren't for everyone.

If you have ever spent time with kids in after school programs, before school programs, during lunch time activities, at camps, or anywhere else, you know that not every child has athletic interests.

Performing arts, chess, art, computers, music and science are some of the more popular, non-athletic interests that kids have today.

It's understandable that some board members, managers and recreation staff aren't interested in offering much more than sports programs. Sports seem to reach higher numbers of participation and registration.

It's Not All about the Numbers

In one small town that I worked for we would have 30 students from each grade level sign-up for soccer. Our non-athletic afterschool enrichment programs were lucky to attract 10 students from three grade levels. For each of those 10 students though, our programs were just what they needed.

I believe it's the duty of youth recreation organizations to offer programs for everyone. Sports are offered by recreation departments, schools, clubs, and various other youth organizations. Athletes are covered. There are plenty of athletic opportunities for our youth.

What we need more of are fitness programs for the non-athletic kids, arts programs (drama, drawing, painting, scrapbooking, magic, etc.), programs that foster creativity, programs that foster thinking and strategy (i.e. chess), etc.

When I run a program that has fewer than 10 participants and I start to doubt if I should be running such a program, I think of the Starfish Story. If you haven't heard the story before, you can find many versions of it on the internet.

The original Starfish Story is by Loren Eiseley. Here is the version I like the best...

The Starfish Story

Once upon a time, there was a wise man that used to go to the ocean to do his writing. He had a habit of walking on the beach before he began his work.

One day, as he was walking along the shore, he looked down the beach and saw a human figure moving like a dancer. He smiled to himself at the thought of someone who would dance to start the day, and so, he walked faster to catch up.

As he got closer, he noticed that the figure was that of a young man, and that what he was doing was not dancing at all. The young man was reaching down to the shore, picking up small objects, and throwing them into the ocean.

He came closer still and called out "Good morning! May I ask what it is that you are doing?"

The young man paused, looked up, and replied "Throwing starfish into the ocean."

"I must ask, then, why are you throwing starfish into the ocean?" asked the somewhat startled wise man.

To this, the young man replied, "The sun is up and the tide is going out. If I don't throw them in, they'll die."

Upon hearing this, the wise man commented, "But, young man, do you not realize that there are miles and miles of beach and there are starfish all along every mile? You can't possibly make a difference!"

At this, the young man bent down, picked up yet another starfish, and threw it into the ocean. As it met the water, he said, "I made a difference to that one!"

Your indoor enrichment program may only get a few participants, but without those programs you may not have had the opportunity to make a difference to those few.

Although making a difference to a select number of kids is enough for most of us to want to offer a program, it may not be enough to convince directors and board members.

Here is a list of benefits that drama programs provide. These are important to know. It is also important that parents understand a few of these benefits as well. Use some of them in your brochure and other marketing materials.

Here are 10 reasons you should be running a drama program…

1. IT'S ENJOYABLE FOR EVERYONE

Have you ever run a class that the kids enjoyed but you dreaded? Drama is one of those programs that everyone seems to enjoy.

Students like drama classes because it's full of games and fun activities, they get to move around and act silly and they get the positive attention that most kids thrive on.

Parents appreciate these drama programs because it gives their children an outlet to express themselves, it's a program their children enjoy going to and the parents get to see their children having a great time during the performance.

Youth leaders really like the program because it is easy to set up and run (especially by having this book). Since it is a program that the kids enjoy it is more fun to run each class.

Have you ever been a part of a class or program where the kids were forced by their parents to attend? It's brutal. Trying to keep the students positively engaged and attempting to keep them well behaved under these conditions can make a youth leader wonder why they didn't become a computer programmer.

2. IT'S A LOW COST PROGRAM

This is music to a director's ears.

Low cost programming makes board members and directors happy indeed. In many cases it also allows an organization to offer more programs.

Let's say you have $10,000 for programs. You can offer an after school film program (they are expensive to start…yikes!) or you can offer a drama program, a volleyball program, a magic program, a chess program, a 5k training program, a dog training clinic, a family bingo night and more.

Of course, a drama program can be more expensive than not if you decide to purchase elaborate props, costumes, set pieces, etc.

Spending a lot of money on props and costumes doesn't make the program better.

All of the low cost, thrift-store costumes, hats, props, etc. that I use for the performances fits nicely into the trunk of my car.

I learned long ago that you don't have to spend a ton of money to make a great enrichment program.

3. Cuts in School Funding

Because of the ongoing cuts in school funding many schools have decreased, and in some cases eliminated, the number of arts programs they offer.

Music, drama and art classes are the first to go during budget cuts.

As a youth organization you have the opportunity to offer the classes and programs that students are missing.

In many cases you can partner with the schools in your area to offer these programs to their students in exchange for a classroom to hold them and a stage for the performance.

4. Anyone Can Do It

Drama is something that is for all ages and abilities.

If your organization and/or community feel it's important to offer inclusion programs, drama is a great way to go.

5. It Helps Kids Find Their Passion

I believe kids should try as many activities as they can to find what they enjoy and are good at.

You may be in the position to offer a wide variety of programs for kids to try. Give them the opportunity you may not have had. Allow them to try new things and find their passions. It will make a difference in many of their lives. Start with a great drama program and go on from there.

It Doesn't Snow in L.A.

I didn't actually touch snow until I was 17 years old, the first time I went skiing. I enjoyed it. I wondered why I hadn't tried it before.

It wasn't until I was 20 that I tried snowboarding. I instantly fell in love with snowboarding. There are a lot of things that I wish I had had the opportunity to try when I was younger: languages, filmmaking, computer programming, guitar, kayaking, wakeboarding, etc. What other kinds of things did I miss out on?

The opportunities I had growing up were probably the same for many of you. They were limited to sports, scouts, band instruments, acting and choir. That leaves a lot of open territory.

---

6. STUDENTS LEARN BETTER COMMUNICATION

Students learn how to project their voice and speak clearly. They learn how to successfully, and unsuccessfully communicate with others. They gain confidence speaking in front of, and with, others.

In short they are learning appropriate ways of communication.

7. STUDENTS USE AND DEVELOP THEIR IMAGINATION

Don't we all need to use our imagination?

- Imagination provides possibilities for everyone.
- In many fields of work it is important to be creative.
- Solving many of life's obstacles uses creativity and imagination.
- Imagination keeps things interesting – it gives life excitement.

Drama promotes the use of imagination and creativity.

8. STUDENTS LEARN TO ACT

As adults it is important to act. We do it every day. Those of us who are good at it have an easier time dealing with others.

When we go to an interview and we are nervous, we ACT confident.

When we are upset and see someone that may be worried, we ACT happy.

When a family member or friend needs someone to talk to, we may not be in the mood to listen or empathize, but we ACT as though we are. After all, they are our family and our friends. We don't want to hurt their feelings.

Acting is a skill that we all use.

9. It's an Opportunity for Students to Grow

Improvisation games and acting in general allows, even demands, that the students put themselves into situations physically, mentally and emotionally that they may not understand at first.

By placing themselves into their character and searching their feelings they gain an understanding of others. They grow as a person.

10. Students Increase Their Confidence

Getting in front of ones peers, not to mention an audience, and stretching to be something or someone else is no easy task for most people.

Actors put themselves out there to be judged. When a student learns the correct way to act, when they learn about posture, breathing, gesturing, speaking clearly, and expressing themselves through their character, and the audience applauds their efforts, it does wonderful things for their confidence. This is why you want to set your students up for success.

You want them to learn, so you'll have to correct your students a lot, but you should find every reason you can to praise them.

Your drama program is not the place to teach kids the harsh realities of critics and naysayers. Make sure your program is a safe place for them to learn and experiment with acting.

These are the lessons that stay with drama students into adulthood.

3

AND...ACTION!

LESSON PLANS

The next few pages have example lesson plans for a 10-week program.

You can use the lesson plans as is or simply use them as outlines for your classes.

The games and activities I have included on the lesson plans can be found in Chapter 5. Each lesson plan is for a 1 hour and 30 minute class. Each class can be scaled back to an hour if need be, but not less than that.

WEEK ONE

Week one is all about laying a foundation for the rest of the program. It's a time when students and leaders get to know each other, ground rules are laid out, expectations are discussed and the students are introduced to the world of acting.

SIGN IN

Have the students sign in. This always helped me to learn their names. It works better for me then a name game.

INTRODUCTIONS

Take a few minutes to allow everyone to introduce themselves, including the leader(s). Each person should state three things:

- Name
- Grade
- Experience if any
- Why they are taking the class
- Favorite (food, movie, cartoon, or whatever)

It helps to write the questions on a board before hand.

WHAT IS DRAMA?

Ask the kids what drama means to them. When each one has answered let them know that they are here to learn the basics of acting.

WHAT ARE YOUR EXPECTATIONS?

Ask the students what they are expecting.

Many times the students will have no idea what to expect. This can worry them and what you want is to develop a safe place for the students to try things out, to stretch themselves.

After each student has had a chance to speak let them all know what to expect over the next 10 weeks.

MY 5 RULES

Here are my five rules that I post on the board before my classes:

- Respect (for others, the leaders, and themselves) This includes putting people down, putting themselves down, and talking over the leader and

- other students.
- Talking Loud (projecting) – When you are "on stage" you should always be projecting your voice. Projecting is not yelling.
- Be on time. Coming in late disrupts the class.

- "Freeze" – If the leader says "freeze" everyone on stage is to do just that. Stop where you are in the position your in. There will always be a good reason for it.

  As a leader you will want to freeze the students so that you can correct their posture, gesture or position on stage.
- Have FUN!

THEATER TERMS

Your students will probably be new to acting. Even if they are not this will be a good review for them. Go over the following terms so that they know what they mean when they hear them:

- Actor positions
  - Full front (facing the audience)
  - Full back (back is to the audience)
  - One quarter right or left (a.k.a. cheating)
  - Three quarters right or left
  - Profile right or left (shoulder is facing the audience – audience sees your profile)
- Character role
- Cue
- Dialogue
- Monologue
- Gesture
- Set
- Prop, or set/stage prop
- Hand prop
- Pantomime
- Sight cue
- Stage areas
  - Upstage (the back of the stage, furthest from the audience)
    - Upstage center
    - Upstage left (actor's left)
    - Upstage right (actor's right)
  - Center Stage
    - Center Stage left
    - Center Stage right
  - Downstage (the front of the stage, closest to the audience)
    - Downstage center

27

- Downstage left
- Downstage right
- Stage left and Stage right (if you tell the actor to exit stage left they will exit to their left, not the audiences)

STAGE AREA

This is a game to make sure they know the areas of the stage.

If you are not working on an actual stage (you're in a classroom for example) tape off an area that represents the stage.

Have all the students go to center stage. When you call an area, all of them are to walk there.

Start giving the class directions; "Upstage left", "Downstage center", "Exit stage right", "Center stage left." Once you think they have got it have them take their seats.

PERFORMANCE ETIQUETTE

- Gesturing – use the hand or arm furthest from the audience. For example, if the actor is pointing towards something that is to the right of them they should use their right hand (the arm furthest from the audience). If they were to point to Stage Right with their left arm their arm would be in front of their face.
- Turning – When an actor turns on stage they should turn towards the audience. Actors should not be showing their back to the audience unless the script calls for it.
- Crossing the Stage – When two or more actors cross a stage the actor closest to the audience should be a step or two back. This is called trailing. The audience should be able to see both actors. If the actors were crossing the stage side by side, then the audience will only be able to see the actor closest to them.
- Facial Expressions – We are doing comedic sketches on stage. Your student's facial expressions should be over the top. Show them different expressions the normal, everyday way (such as happy, mad, and surprised), and then show them the expressions in an over the top, comedic way. Really over do it. The students will get a laugh and you will get your point across. You are looking to entertain our audience on the evening of your performance. Make them laugh. Go big.

GROUPS

Break into groups of no more than 5 students per group

THEATER GAME/ACTIVITY
Solo Pantomimes (pg. 51)

THEATER GAME/ACTIVITY
Where Am I? (pg. 57)

INTRODUCE ONE SKETCH
You may not have the time for this. If you do, have the students sit down. Hand them a script to one of the sketches (you will hand out the notebooks at the next class). Read over the script with the students. This should whet their appetite for the next class session.

Q & A
Answer any questions the student may have and remember to give them praise for their work today.

CLEAN UP AND GO

WEEK TWO

This class will be a bit more engaging than the last. This class will be about games, acting, and an introduction to the sketches you have chosen to use.

SIGN IN
Have the students sign in.

REVIEW

My 5 Rules (post on the board before class):

- Respect (for others, the leaders, and themselves)
- Talking Loud (projecting)
- Be on time.
- "Freeze"
- Have FUN!

Drama Terms
- Actor positions
  - Full front
  - Full back
  - One quarter right or left
  - Three quarters right or left
  - Profile right or left
- Character role
- Cue
- Dialogue
- Monologue
- Gesture
- Set
- Prop, or set/stage prop
- Hand prop
- Pantomime
- Sight cue
- Stage areas
  - Upstage
    - Upstage center
    - Upstage left (actor's left)
    - Upstage right (actor's right)
    - Center Stage left

- Center Stage right
  - Downstage
    - Downstage center
    - Downstage left
    - Downstage right
  - Stage left and Stage right
- Performance Etiquette
  - Gestures
  - Turns
  - Crossing the Stage
  - Facial Expressions

THEATER GAME/ACTIVITY
Pantomiming Emotions (pg. 52)

GOOD STAGE VOICE
Discuss what a good stage voice is.

- Rate of Speed – Many beginners talk too fast when they are on stage. Unless noted, their characters speak at the same rate of speed as a normal person. We want to make sure the audience hears every part of our dialogue. If we are talking too fast the audience may miss something. (As a leader you will need to remind some of them of this as they are acting. Simply tell them to slow down.)
- Projection – This is one you will probably have to remind them of constantly. Most beginners will speak too softly. That's alright if you are on television where they have microphones everywhere. On stage, however, the actors must speak up and be heard. Tell them that too many sketches have been ruined because the audience couldn't hear the funny parts. You don't want this to happen to your performance.
- Clarity – It is very important to speak clearly. Again, you may have to remind student of this as they rehearse or play the drama games. Mumbling won't cut it for most roles.

THEATER GAME/ACTIVITY
What Are You Doing? (pg. 58)

THEATER GAME/ACTIVITY
Color the Phrase (pg. 53)

INTRODUCE THE SKITS
For the rest of the class have the students sit around a table, or you can move

the chairs to form a circle. This is only a reading.

- Pass out the student notebooks.

They will get to keep them as long as they remember to bring them to each class.

If you do not think they will remember, collect them at the end of class.

- Assign students parts to read. Let them know that you are not handing out parts; you are simply choosing readers so they can get a feel of the sketch.
- Go over as many sketches as you can.
- Let them know that they should start thinking about the roles they want to play.

Next week you will be assigning their roles. Let them know that not everyone will get all the roles they want, but you will try to be as fair as possible.

WEEK THREE

During this class session you will be assigning roles to each of the students.

Let's review that a bit more.

You can hold auditions if you would like. If the students are in middle school then it would be appropriate so that they get the chance to experience what it's like to audition. If the kids are in elementary school then I would simply find out what roles each person is interested in and assign them as fairly as you can.

Each student should have at least one lead or co-lead role. This is why it's great to have a program where the performance is a series of sketches.

Try and make sure that each student is in the same number of sketches as everyone else. I use a graph like the one below:

	The Director	Wet Box	Rhythm	Echo
Sandy	L	S		S
Brianna	L	S	S	
Scott	S		L	S
Chad	L		S	S
Sherry		S	S	L
Cathleen	L	S	S	
Nick	S	L		S
Lauren	S	L	S	
L = Lead Role S = Supporting Role				

By using a graph, which is a spreadsheet I print off of Excel, I can see that everyone has at least one lead role and everyone is in three sketches. Of course, this is only an example. You may have more sketches and possibly more students, although a minimum of eight students is what I will run a drama program with.

Now, let's go onto the lesson.

Sᴉɢɴ Iɴ

Have the students sign in.

REVIEW MY 5 RULES

I will ask if anyone broke the rules last week.

Many times a few of the students will say that they did. It's usually something like they put themselves down or spoke while the leader was speaking.

I let them know that this is a new week, a clean slate.

OTHER REVIEWS

If you feel you need to review anything than do so.

I will make notes during the previous class session on what we will need to review the following week. There is always something.

Sometimes I will quiz them individually. "Jessie, show me Center Stage Left." "Gloria, stand Center Stage and point towards Stage Right. Class what is she doing right?"

NOTEBOOKS

Pass out the notebooks or make sure they have brought their.

 I always keep a few extra notebooks on hand in case someone has forgotten theirs.

WHO DO YOU WANT TO BE?

Now it's time to find out what roles the students want to play.

On the next page you'll see the form I pass out to the students. I ask them to fill it out and hand it back to me.

PAPER BAG SKITS

Break the students up into groups and give them a paper bag with 5 or 6 items each.

The items should be random things. For example, one bag may have the following items:

- Hacky Sack
- Spoon
- Stapler
- Lifesavers
- Floss

The next bag may have:

- Newspaper article
- Shoelace
- Packet of hot sauce
- Pencil
- Deck of cards

The groups will now be given five to ten minutes to come up with a skit. They have to use all the items in the bag.

Occasionally, I will give them a phrase they will have to use as well. For example, I may have them use one of these phrases "That's hogwash", "My diapers are soiled", or "Aye, Aye Captain!" If you do this make sure that all the groups use the same phrase.

ASSIGN ROLES

While the students prepare their paper bag their skits I will go through the role requests.

Using my blank graph, I assign roles. I first look at each student first choice. If I feel they would be good in that role I will assign it to them. If I don't think it's a good fit for them I will go on to their second choice.

If I have only eight to ten students than they may all get two of their top three requests for leads.

Keep in mind that you won't please everyone.

Take in account what's best for the performance and what roles the students want to play.

Make sure everyone gets a lead or two and have a few supporting roles.

Before you "post" the roles let the students know that some of them may be disappointed, and that unfortunately it's a part of acting. Not everyone will get the roles they wanted. Overall, however, everyone should be more or less pleased that they got at least one or two lead roles.

Role Requests

Name: _____

The Lead Roles that I would like to play are:

1st Choice _____
2nd Choice _____
3rd Choice _____

The Supporting Roles that I would like to play are:

1st Choice _____
2nd Choice _____
3rd Choice _____

Role Requests

Name: _____

The Lead Roles that I would like to play are:

1st Choice _____
2nd Choice _____
3rd Choice _____

The Supporting Roles that I would like to play are:

1st Choice _____
2nd Choice _____
3rd Choice _____

PAPER BAG SKIT PERFORMANCES

Have the groups perform their Paper Bag Skits.

POST STUDENT ROLES

Inform or post the results for the Role Requests.

 If you need more time have the groups exchange paper bags and give them 5 more minutes to prepare a new skit.

Once the students have found out what roles they are playing have them highlight their parts in their notebooks.

GO OVER THE SKETCHES

The students will be anxious to act.

Use the rest of the class time to have them go over the sketches. Go over one sketch at a time.

Choose a sketch, have the actors take the stage and then guide them through it.

As a director you will have a vision as to how you want to see the sketch take place. In order to do that you will need to direct. Let them know what they are doing right and what they need to correct. Help them envision where they are and who their characters are.

- Are the actors positioned properly on the stage?
- Are they using proper gestures?
- Can you hear and understand the dialogue?
- Can you see all the actors on stage?
- Are they acting - or are they merely being themselves while reading the lines?

Go easy on the students, but lay the groundwork.

This needs to be a positive experience. Encourage them to go big, to the point of over-acting a bit. These are comedic sketches.

Above all, make sure you and the students are having fun.

WEEKS FOUR - EIGHT

The following five weeks will be more or less the same format; drama games for one-third of the class, rehearsing of the sketches for the next two-thirds, ending with one favorite drama game.

If, during the last couple of weeks, the students have really nailed down the sketches and are ready to perform, then by all means play more drama games. You will still want to rehearse the sketches, but the class should be more like one-third drama games, one-third rehearing, and one-third more drama games.

You can easily add two more weeks to this program making it a 12 week class. Simply add two more of these lesson plans.

SIGN IN

Have the students sign in.

REVIEW MY 5 RULES

Make sure there are consequences for not following the rules. For example, if a student is not projecting have them go outisde and do their lines loud enough for everyone inside to hear. Better yet, take the whole class outside and have some of the students stand a fair distance away to see if they can hear the actors.

OTHER REVIEWS

Review anything else that may need reviewing.

THEATER GAME/ACTIVITY

Choose from the list in chapter 5 or a few of your own.

REHEARSE SKETCHES

Rehearse, rehears, reheasrs so the studetns are well prepared before they get in front of an audience.

THEATER GAME/ACTIVITY

The students may have a favorite. Play it as a reward for behaving and giving a great effort during the rehearsals.

WEEK NINE

This week is about all about rehearsing for the performance.

If you are able to get access to the stage or area where you will be performing for the student's friends and family then that would be ideal. If not, that's okay, you'll just need to have everyone imagine that they are on stage and to treat it as such. That means that after they have exited the stage they need to stay up there "behind the curtain", instead of sitting down to watch the others. In other words, treat it like it was the actual performance.

SIGN IN

Have the students sign in.

REVIEW MY 5 RULES

Don't write them on the board and see if they remember what the rules are.

THEATER GAME/ACTIVITY

Play a warm-up drama game/activity.

PERFORMANCE SCHEDULE

Give each student a copy of the performance schedule. This is something you will need to prepare ahead of time. A sample is on page 35.

BACK STAGE

Have the students go "Back Stage", behind the curtains.

There should be no talking. This should be treated as though it is the actual performance. If the students are talking "Back Stage" now, they will most likely be talking "Back Stage" the night of the performance.

REHEARSE

Run through the performance. Make sure that you correct the students when you need to and praise them often.

Keep in mind projection, rate and clarity of dialogue.

PROPS

During the last 20 minutes of class talk about what props and costumes you and the students would like to see.

All the props I use for my performances will literally fit in one large storage tub. You can have more than that or less. Frankly, the family and friends will be at the performance to support the students. They will love the performance, props or no props. Of course, it makes things more interesting and fun if you have at lest a few props.

 After you have made a list of what you need there are a few ways you can get props:

1. Ask the students to bring them from home or to buy them by next week.
2. Email parents the list and ask if they would help get the props needed for their children's performance.
3. Search thrift shops, discount stores, the internet, etc. and purchase them yourself.
4. Make the props.
5. A combination of the suggestions above.

A SAMPLE PERFORMANCE SCHEDULE

Welcoming the Audience – Sherry (this is the leader of the class…you)

Introductions – Sherry and the Exit Stage Left Performers
(or whatever you decided to call the group of actors)

(Curtain)

Emergency Broadcast System – Everyone

(Curtain)

The Elevator – Michelle, Holly, Frank, Lori, Brian

(Curtain)

Rhythm – Sue, Bobby, Billy, Sally, Jean, Max

(Curtain)

Mixed Up Magic – Jeff and Andrea

(Curtain)

Mosquitoes – Dana, Ed, Heather, Jim, Austin, Jackie

(Curtain)

The Pick Pocket – Tom and Jerry

(Curtain)

The Doctor's Office – Jamie, Tina, Dawnelle, Colin, Todd, Lisa

(Curtain)

The Director – Everyone

(Curtain)

Curtain Call

(Curtain)

Photos

(Curtain)

Thank the audience for coming – Sherry

Do not leave without cleaning up first!

WEEK 10

The final week is for dress rehearsal. Use the stage that the students will be performing on. This is your last chance to rehearse and work out all the kinks.

SIGN IN

Have the students sign in.

GATHER PROPS

Gather all the props and costumes and place them Back Stage where they will be the most accessible for the performers.

Props and costumes should be used for this rehearsal.

REHEARSE

Run through the whole program with little or no interruption.

Of course, if you need to make changes or corrections do so. Don't start a whole sketch over again because someone forgot a line.

A LOOK BACK

At the end of the class session sit all the students down in a circle and discuss the last 10 weeks with them.

Talk about how far they have come and how proud you are of them. Open it up for comments, questions, verbal "pats on the back", etc.

SNACKS

If you would like, bring some snacks to share or have a pizza party to cap off the class.

With the exception of my Harry Potter program, this is the only after school program I do this for.

If for some reason you have the performance before this final week (I'll occasionally have my performance a week before this class due to stage accessibility) a pizza party feels like an after-show cast party.

4

IT'S SHOWTIME
THE PERFORMANCE

This chapter is intended to cover all the things you will need to do to get ready for and put on a successful performance. At the end of the chapter there is a check-off list for your use.

ONE OR TWO WEEKS BEFORE THE PERFORMANCE

INVITE

Invite parents to the performance.

 Either create an attractive evite (email invitation) or send them an invitation by mail. I like to get special invitations from my local party supply store.

Let parents know that it would be great if they brought other family and friends. The bigger the audience the better.

SNACKS

Email parents to ask them to bring a snack item for the play.

Not only will this save you time and money of buying snacks, but everyone has different tastes. If each family brings a dish then everyone is covered and there's more of a community feel about it.

DRESS REHEARSAL

Do a dress rehearsal on the stage you will be using.

Make sure you go through the whole performance exactly how you want it to happen. Work out those last minute kinks and snafus.

STUDENT EXPECTATIONS

Make it clear to the students what is expected of them and how they should behave on the night of the performance.

ONE TO TWO HOURS BEFORE THE PERFORMANCE

SNACK TABLE

Set up the table for snacks.

 I have a sign I bought from a party supply store that says "Concessions". I tape this above the table.

ADVERTISE

Put out flyers and other information for upcoming programs. What better place to advertise your future classes than here, amongst satisfied clients?

Decorate

Decorate the area if you want. I have paper signs that look like street signs. They say "Broadway", "42nd Street", etc. I also got these from a party supply store.

Props

Place all of your props back stage.

Check Curtain

Open and close the curtain to make sure it's not stuck or not working.

Check Lighting

If you are using lighting, check to make sure they are working.

Script Copies

Make sure you have copies of the scripts back stage so if an actor forgets a line you, or an assistant, can feed it to them from off stage.

Round 'Em Up

When the students arrive have them begin to gather Back Stage.

Get Help

Ask your oldest and/or most mature students to be your helpers today. They will usually take this responsibility very seriously and will keep the others in line if things start getting chaotic.

These responsible students are also the ones you want working the curtain and helping with the costumes and props if you do not have an adult assistant with you.

Restrooms

Make sure that only one student is allowed to go to the restroom at a time. For some reason, once everyone is Back Stage, students want to go to the restroom in groups.

Parents want to know that you are in control. They do not want to see groups of kids wandering around right before the show.

As a director you certainly don't want to have to go looking for actors before the show.

Also, let the actors know that they are not to go to the restroom during the performance.

POST THE SCHEDULE

Post the show schedule in a few obvious spots so that the actors can see which sketch is next.

MUSIC

Cue any music you might have.

TEN MINUTES BEFORE THE PERFORMANCE

PEP TALK

Gather the actors together and give them a little pep talk. Tell them how proud you are of the work they've put into this. They WILL be nervous.

RELAX AND FOCUS

Have them do some relaxation techniques, such as taking deep breaths. This will help calm their nerves and focus them on the show.

You may find that the kids are so amped up and excited that they are running around back stage in a panicked frenzy. Focusing their attention and calming them down will work wonders for your sanity and theirs.

EVERYTHING IN IT'S PLACE

Have an assistant or student make sure that all props, costumes and/or sound effects are in their proper place.

DURING THE PERFORMANCE

INTRODUCE YOURSELF

Before the show starts go on stage and introduce yourself and your organization.

LET THEM KNOW

Let the parents know what an honor it was to work with their children. Thank them for the snacks they brought. "And now...on with the show.

During your introduction, you might want to take a moment to inform the parents of any upcoming classes they may be interested in. Let them know that they can find more information on the back table.

INTRODUCE THE SKETCHES

Before each sketch have a student go out and introduce it. "Ladies and Gentlemen, this sketch (or skit) is called The Director."

Another way to introduce your sketches is to make nice signs that can be read by the entire audience. The student would then walk out with the sign and say nothing. As the curtain opens the student walks off.

AFTER THE PERFORMANCE

CURTAIN CALL

It's time for the Curtain Call. Open the curtain and introduce each actor one at a time. You should be doing this from behind the curtain, or an assistant can do the actor introductions from on stage.

As they come on stage they will line up next to each other. Once they are all on stage the group will hold hands and take a few bows together.

Then you, the director, will walk on stage in front of them and take a bow. The actors applaud you at this time as well as the audience.

Make certain you practice this during the dress rehearsal.

AWARDS (OPTIONAL, BUT WORTH IT.)

After the bows, encourage the parents to have a seat. Let them know that you have a few more things to say.

Briefly talk about each student and give them an award.

"This actress blew me away with how quickly she picked up the art of acting, I am so proud of her efforts. The award for Most Improved Actor goes to Amanda."

Parents and students will love the extra effort you put into making the performance an awards show as well. Below are a few examples of awards categories. I'm sure you can think of others.

- Funniest Character

- Pure Talent
- Star Performer
- Go Getter
- Greatest Little Ball of Energy
- Best Helper
- Best Friend
- Mother Hen
- I'm the Leader
- Risk Taker
- Princess
- I Love to Act

PHOTO OP

Get the group together and let the parents know that this is a photo opportunity.

I can't tell you how many times I've seen parents try to get everyone together after the show has finished. Make it easy on them.

THE DISHES

Remind the parents to take home any dishes they may have brought.

SCHMOOZE

While everyone is snacking be available to speak with the student's family and friends. Thank them for coming.

Take a Bow, You Did It!

ACTION PLAN

The following action plan should be used to make sure that you haven't forgotten anything leading up to your performance.

One to two weeks prior…

- ☐ Invite parents and their family and friends.
- ☐ Ask parents to bring a snack.
- ☐ Hold a dress rehearsal.
- ☐ Let students know what's expected of them.

Night of the performance…

- ☐ Set up snack table.
- ☐ Put out flyers.
- ☐ Decorate.
- ☐ Place props Back Stage.
- ☐ Make sure curtain works properly.
- ☐ Make sure lights work properly.
- ☐ Make sure you have scripts Back Stage.
- ☐ Gather the actors.
- ☐ Give them a pep talk.
- ☐ Have the actors relax and focus. Deep breathes.
- ☐ Make sure everything's in its place.

5

LET'S PLAY

15 OF MY FAVORITE THEATER GAMES/ACTIVITIES

These games and activities have been favorites of my students. Most of these games are for beginners. A few of them are for intermediate acting students and will be indicated as such.

There are many, many more games and activities that you can do with your class. In the Resources section you will find suggestions for other books that have more games. You can find theater game books on Amazon or at your local library.

SOLO PANTOMIMES

Students get the opportunity to pantomime a scene while the rest of the class tries to guess what they are doing. Write out activities on index cards ahead of time.

- Pass out an index card that has an activity written on it to each student.
- Give them all a few minutes to think about what they are going to do. This should be done silently. No talking.
- Inform the class that they are not to guess until the actor has finished his or her scene.
- Have the first student get in front of the class and act out the activity on the card.
- Once they done allow the other students to guess.
- Let the student know what he or she did well and how they can improve.

Below is a list of activities that you may want to use.

Washing a car
Climbing a huge mountain
Setting up a tent at a campsite
Playing fetch with a dog
Learning to surf
Playing with a remote controlled vehicle
Riding on a rollercoaster
Pretending to be a cowboy in the Wild West
Riding a horse
Playing a board game
Playing Bingo
Getting ready for bed
Falling asleep in class and being caught by the teacher
Playing hide and go seek
Learning to snowboard
Playing paintball
Cooking
Winning a trophy or medal
Winning an Academy Award
Playing dodgeball
Working out

PANTOMIMING EMOTIONS

This is a great introduction to acting out emotions. Simply have the students act out the emotion that is required. Before you get started talk about situations that might bring about the emotion. Having the student imagining themselves in that situation on order to bring about the emotion can be a very good tool for them.

What situations might bring about anger? A friend telling other kids your secret? A bully? When your parents don't let you play video games? It can be different for everyone.

- Have a couple of students stand in front of the class.
- Give them a few emotions to pantomime.
- If they are having trouble, ask them to think of a time they might have felt that emotion. Have them go back to that incident.

Below is a list of emotions.

energetic
lethargic
depressed
happy
excited
angry
perturbed
annoyed
disgusted
jealous
serene
scared
indifferent
lonely
bored
in love
embarrassed
shy
heart broken

COLORING

To color something means to express it in a way other than neutral. For example, I might tell one of my students to repeat the phrase "I love to go to the ice cream store on a hot day." I will say it in a neutral tone. I will ask my students to color it angry. The student will then say the phrase angrily. They have colored the phrase.

The following two games have to do with coloring.

COLOR THE PHRASE

- Have four or five students stand in front of the class.
- Give them a phrase. It can be anything, but I have included a few phrases below.
    - I'm so excited. My family and I are going to Hawaii for vacation.
    - Being on a sailboat makes me seasick.
    - My favorite animal is a billy goat. I like their little beards.
    - I was given a pot of gold by a leprechaun yesterday. I'm rich.
- Have them color it. A list of color options is at the bottom of the page.
- Have each group of students color one phrase in different ways. For example have them say one of the phrases listed softly, then harshly, then excitedly, then while they are crying, and finally as though they are falling asleep.
- Have the next group color a different phrase in five new ways.

COLOR THE NURSERY RHYME

This is the same game except that the group colors a nursery rhyme. Write a short nursery rhyme, or the first few lines or so of a longer one, on the board. Then follow the directions from Color the Phrase.

angry	happy	sad	crazy
cold	hot	crying	laughing
dying	nervous	tired	relaxed
embarrassed	suspicious	secretive	loony
harsh	soft	smooth	suave
confident	cocky	stuck up	goofy
robot	operatic	rock star	blues
hip hop	depressed	two year old	twitch
intelligent	Star Wars	hiding	super hero

ACTING OUT NURSERY RHYMES

Get yourself a good book of nursery rhymes. A book of fairy tales would work as well.

- Choose a nursery rhyme (or fairy tale).
- Assign characters of the story to some of the students to act out.
- Have one of the students read a nursery rhyme. They should read it with feeling. Depending on the students it may be better if you, the instructor, read it.
- As the story is being read the students act out what is being read (and what isn't). The actors are pantomiming, no sound.

Help the students become better actors by suggesting movements, more emotion, proper blocking of a scene (can the audience see everyone?), etc.

This is a fun activity that kids love to do.

Try to get someone who is a good reader to read the story. If you don't know who is good just ask, "Who would like to read a story out loud?" Students who are not the best readers will slow the action down and will be embarrassed in front of the class.

If the kids are younger then it may be best if you read the story.

EMOTIONAL BOUNDARIES

This is an intermediate game. This game will test the students' ability to change emotions instantly. Before you start this game you will need to tape off three sections on the ground. Each section represents a different emotion.

Stage Left	Center Stage	Stage Right
SAD	EXCITED	CONFUSED

Make sure you assign three very different emotions to each section. As the students move around the stage they must match their emotion with the emotion of the section.

- Set the scene or situation, or have the other students set it. This will be improv for the actors.
- Ask two or three of the students to "take the stage".
- Inform the actors that they control the scene since it is improv. As they mover around the stage they are to match the emotion of that area of the stage as indicated by the tape.
- Ask them not to stay in a section too long as that defeats the purpose and fun of the game.
- Give the actors time to do a scene and explore the different areas of the stage.

WALKING TALL

During this game the students will walk around the room as a particular character or with a particular emotion.

1. Have the whole group – or at least half of them – get up and begin walking in a circle around the room.
2. Call out a character or emotion. Students should be walking as that character or with that emotion.

    Here are some examples:

Characters	Emotions
Bodybuilder	Angry
Klutz	Sad
A Bully	Excited
Stuck-Up	Repressing Anger
Police Officer	Tired
Hip Hop Artist	Disgusted
Crazy Person	Adventurous
Spy	Afraid
Lottery Winner	Bored
Court Jester	Fearful
Had Too Much to Eat	Giggly
A Very Old Person	With Peace of Mind
A Child Learning to Walk	In Love
Dancer	In Shock

3. Have the students go big. A person coming in the room should be able to tell how each of them are feeling by the way they are walking.
4. Point out what they are doing with their posture, their head, etc.

WHERE AM I?

In this game a student gets in front of the class and begins acting out, in silence, a character in a certain place. As the other students realize where the actor is he/she gets up and plays a different character in the scene.

1. Choose a student and secretly give them a place to be. Below are examples of places.
2. Let them choose the character that would best show that place.
3. Inform the class that this is a silent activity. They should all pantomime.
4. Also, let them know that once they have figured out where the place is they should raise their hand.
5. Once they are called upon they can "take the stage" and should play a character in the scene that is different from everyone else. For example, if the place is a beach and the main actor is acting as a child who is building a sandcastle, the other students may take parts as a lifeguard, surfer, someone putting on sunscreen, etc.
6. Give the main actor 15-20 seconds before allowing other students to get up and act with them.
7. If you feel that certain students are acting out characters not in line with the place, have them take a seat and watch. For example, a student, seeing the actor portray a child building a sand castle, may think that she is carving a pumpkin. He may then go up "on stage" and start trick-or-treating. Have him sit down and if he insists that he knows it he can whisper it in you ear. You can then tell him if he is correct or not.
8. Once most of the class is up "on stage" then ask them all to tell them where they are. Hopefully they will all say, "The beach."
9. Let everyone have a chance to start a scene.

Places

Baseball Game	Grocery Store	Circus
Wedding	School	Movie Theater
Crashing Plane	On a Rollercoaster	Theme Park
Film Set	Olympics	Rodeo
Photo Shoot	Hotel	Health Club
Spa	Camping	Dentist's Office

WHAT ARE YOU DOING?

This is a popular game that students love to play.

1. The first student gets up in front of the class.
2. The leader gives the student an action to perform (i.e. washing the dog).
3. The student begins acting like he or she is, in this case, washing a dog.
4. The next student comes up and asks the first what he or she is doing, "What are you doing?"
5. The first student responds by saying something other than what they are actually doing, "I'm acting like a monkey."
6. The second student takes on the action that the first student said. So now the first student sits down and the second student begins acting like a monkey.
7. The next student comes up and asks, "What are you doing?"
8. Instead of saying they are acting like a monkey they may say, "I am practicing my ballet."
9. This goes on until everyone has had a chance to play.

Example:

Student #1	(acting like a child running a lemonade stand)
Student #2	What are you doing?
Student #1	Watching a scary movie.
Student #1	(leaves the "stage")
Student #2	(acts as though she is watching a scary movie)
Student #3	(enters the "stage") What are you doing?
Student #2	Fishing, and I just caught a big one.
Student #2	(leaves the "stage")
Student #3	(acts as though he is fishing and is reeling in a huge fish)
Student #4	(enters the "stage") What are you doing?
Student #3	I'm a sumo wrestler getting ready for my next match.
Student #3	(leaves the "stage")
Student #4	(acts as though she is a sumo wrestler preparing for the next match)

1 – 20

This is a great activity that stresses the importance of not talking over other actors while on stage. The idea is to count to twenty without talking at the same time.

1. Gather the group in a circle.
2. Inform the group that the object is to count to twenty as a group. However, if two or more students talk at the same time the group must start over. You can not cheat by going in a circle or pointing at people to say a number.
3. If the students are a little confused they will catch on as soon as you start.
4. The leader starts by saying, "One."
5. Anybody in the group can say, "Two", and so on until you get to 20, but if two players say the same number the group starts back at one.

This game is more difficult then it sounds.

At some point the students will begin to feel when someone is going to talk. They should be looking at each other for some cues (deep breathes, facial expressions that indicate the person is about to speak, a look, etc.)

Talk to students about the importance of not talking over one another.

You want the audience able to understand all the dialogue and not miss anything. If actors are talking over each other when they are not supposed to it makes it very difficult for an audience to follow the scene.

Variation: If some of the students are not saying a number and/or other students are taking over the game by saying most of the numbers, I will add another rule. Everyone must say at least one (or two) number(s).

ONE WORD STORY

Here's a fun and fairly easy game that you can play with beginning and intermediate students.

1. Have the group sit in a circle.
2. Use one word as the start of a story.
3. Go around the circle allowing each student to add one word to the story.
4. Continue and see if the group can come up with a coherent story.
5. You'll have students say words that don't go with the story. That's okay, keep it going. If the student is blatantly trying to ruin the game send them outside for a couple of minutes.

Here's an example of this game:

Teacher:	There
Johnny:	once
Susan:	was
Lisa:	a
Ronald:	kid
Tiffany:	who
Tyson:	was
Jason:	always
Jennifer:	wearing
Teacher:	a
Johnny:	colorful
Susan:	shirt.

The story continues on until it comes to an end on its own or as time permits. Half of the fun – and sometimes frustration – comes from a student saying something different than the person after them thought they would say.

Try to keep things moving.

Do not allow a student to take 30 seconds to think of the right word. If they are having difficulty, go on to the next person. They'll get another turn when it comes around again.

TAXI CAB (A.K.A. HITCHHIKER)

Here's an improv game that kids love to play. It's best played by older kids (middle and high school ages).

1. Set up four chairs; one driver and three passengers.
2. Choose a student
3. The "driver" starts off by pantomiming as though he is driving.
4. The first student acts as though she is hailing a cab from the curb (or hitchhiking).
5. The driver pantomimes stopping. The first student gets in the back seat.
6. The passenger plays the role of a very specific personality. Below are some examples. The passenger tells the cab driver where she needs to go.
   - A surfer
   - A woman in labor
   - An old man that wants to tell his life story
   - A secret agent
   - A British rock star
   - A pompous actor
   - A Valley girl
   - A cartoon voice actor
   - A cute child
   - A vain bodybuilder
   - A pirate
   - A Wild West cowboy

If the students have a hard time coming up with a good character give them an index card with a character on it for them to portray.

7. The cab driver takes on the personality of his passenger as he drivers the passenger to her destination.
8. Let this continue for a minute and then have another student hail the cab.
9. The new passenger gets in with a completely different personality, and now the cab driver and the first passenger take on the new passenger's traits.
10. This continues until the cab is full (a driver and three passengers).
11. The cab driver then begins dropping off his passengers starting from the last one that got in the cab.
12. As the passengers get out of the cab everyone switches to the personality of the next passenger to be dropped off.
13. Once all the passengers are out of the cab the cab driver goes back to his original personality.

This game gives your students good practice at playing different characters. For younger kids you may want to give them a character to potray.

FREEZE TAG

This is one of the most popular theater improv games around. Just about every-one who has ever taken an improv and/or theater class has played Freeze Tag.

- Have two students stand in front of the class.
- Ask the other students to suggest a scene or situation for the actors to improvise.
- Once you have a good suggestion the two students in front of the class will act out the scene.
- After a giving the actors a little time to improv allow any of the other students to jump in when they are ready. This is done by the student yelling, "Freeze."
- Once the two actors hear "freeze" they must stop all action and dialogue and hold the position they are in.
- The student who yelled "Freeze" will come up, tag one of the actors and take his or her place, matching the actor's pose. The chosen actor now sits down with the rest of the students.
- The new actor must now change the scene entirely based on the pose he or she is in. For example, if the frozen actor was lying on the floor stretched out like Superman, the student taking his place may start the new scene by swimming across a pool.
- Once the two have had a minute or so to do their scene the next student yells, "Freeze", and takes the place, and matches the pose, of the other actor.
- Try to get all the students to take a turn or two.

Variation: The leader is the one who yells "Freeze" and both actors are replaced by two students.

FIRST AND LAST LINE

This is an intermediate game. The actors must improv a scene using a specific line of dialogue to start the scene and using another specific line of dialogue to end the scene. Scenes should not be very long, a couple of minutes tops.

- Have a few players "take the stage".
- Ask the other students for a first line and a last line.
- Give the actors a few seconds to decide who is going to deliver the first line and who is going to deliver the last line.
- The students can then act out any scene they want as long as they use the two lines.

When running improv games, there seems to be two schools of thought by instructors.

The first is that the games end on their own no matter how long they go.

The second is that the students have a certain amount of time.

Personally, I like to give the students a certain amount of time. I don't tell the students they have x amount of minutes, but I do let them know that the scene is running a little long by saying "Wrap it up."

PARTY QUIRKS

This is an intermediate game. Here's a game made famous by the hit TV show Whose Line Is It Anyways? I had one group of students that begged me to run this game at every class.

- Choose one student to leave the room out of earshot.
- Choose three students to be the "party guests".
- Ask the other students to suggest quirks for the party guests. Each party guest should have a completely different quirk. Here are some suggestions to get you started:
  - Circus performer
  - Thinks they are the Terminator
  - A superhero
  - A specific character that everyone would know (Sponge Bob, Hannah Montana, Yoda, etc.)
  - One of the school's teachers or the principal
  - A type of athlete (football player, boxer, bowler, etc.)
  - An alien
- Once each guest has their quirk, or character, bring back the student who was outside. They are the party host.
- The game starts with the party host getting ready for the party (putting out snacks, turning on music, etc.).
- The doorbell rings and the host opens the imaginary door for the first guest.
- They greet each other and the guest acts out their quirk as they enjoy the party.
- Each guest is introduced to the scene by the sound of the doorbell.
- Whenever the host thinks he or she knows someone's quirk they should say it in a way that is part of the scene. Instead of saying, "You think you're the Terminator", the host may say something like, "It's a little scary having you here. I mean a robot from the future going around killing people is a bit disturbing. You should at least change your name. Terminator is a scary name. How about Bob?"
- Once the host has guessed a quirk correctly that guest leaves the scene and sits with the audience.

Let the class know ahead of time that the host should not just stand there and guess. They should be playing host by introducing guests to each other, replenishing snacks, having conversations with their guests, etc. The guest should go big with their quirks since the whole idea of the game is to get the host to guess their bizarre behavior.

VACATION SLIDESHOW

This is an intermediate game. This drama game is a lot of fun. Students need to improv quickly, but they won't have to speak.

Imagine you are telling the class about a recent vacation you went on. In fact, you are going to show them a slide show of it.

The vacation pictures or "slides" will be two to four students acting out you and your family or friends.

1. Tell the class that you are going to tell them about your latest vacation and that a few of students will act out the pictures.
2. Have a few of the students get up in front of the class.
3. You (the teacher) start off by telling the class where you went. For example, "Ok class on my vacation I went to Hawaii. I'm going to show you a slide show, some pictures of my trip."
4. Next describe the first slide. "Here I am with my two best friends and we are hiking up a volcano."
5. The students strike a pose of what the picture may look like. They hold the pose until you go onto the next slide. In our example the students might pantomime hiking up a hill and being very tired.
6. "Oh, this next picture shows me and my best friend surfing. If you look closely you'll see a shark in the corner of the picture." For this slide two of the students would be surfing. Maybe one of them is falling off the surfboard. The other student might be in the background as a shark.
7. Continue the slide show for a few more pictures. Then have a few new students do the same thing but this time you should change the vacation location. "Here I am with my parents at Disneyland…"

6

PLAN IT AND THEY WILL COME...WELL, NOT EXACTLY

20 CREATIVE MARKETING IDEAS TO FILL YOUR CLASS

It's not easy to get registrations for a new program. Even when a program is established new students need to know about it.

In this chapter you will find 20 marketing ideas that go beyond your brochure or catalog of classes. The first 10 are designed to get the word out for a new program. The next 10 are to market an existing program.

10 IDEAS TO GET THE WORD OUT ABOUT YOUR FIRST DRAMA CLASS

PRESS RELEASES - WHILE NOT VERY CREATIVE, THEY ARE EFFECTIVE

Writing a press release for the local paper can work wonders for creating a buzz about your drama program.

Unfortunately, many parents will get your catalog and either skim through it, missing half of the information, or just toss it in the trash. Those same parents may be reading the newspaper and see the article about your new drama program.

Relying solely on the brochure or catalog may not get youth registrations you need to run a drama program.

She Doesn't Read the Brochure

After the performance of one of my classes a parent started talking with me. She said the usual kind things about how her daughter loved the class, and how the performance was so cute.

She then went on to tell me that if it weren't for her mother, the student's grandmother, reading about it in the local newspaper, she would not have known about it. She admitted to me that she never looks at the brochure is sent out to all the city residents. She figured all of our programs were for little kids and older adults.

I informed her that we offered classes for all ages.

This is one example of someone who didn't look at the brochure/catalog. She's not the only one. I've had plenty of parents come up to me over the years telling me that they would not have known about the program if it weren't for the marketing the recreation department did outside of the brochure and website.

If you have someone in your office that does press releases already, write them up a paragraph or two about your program and have them turn it into a press release that they will send to the paper.

If, however, you have to write a press release yourself, don't worry it's pretty easy. Google "how to write a press release" and you will see free articles about how to do it.

I'm on T.V.

Do you know about public access TV?

Did you know that anybody can produce a 30 minute or one hour show and have it air on public access TV?

It's true.

In the next chapter I discuss how this is done. For now, all you need to know is that it is possible. If you are motivated you can have your class perform on screen.

The excitement of being on TV is sure to attract a number of kids to your program.

Many parents will be excited about the possibility as well, even if it is only public access.

Once you have ensured that it can happen at your local public access station and you are willing to do the legwork to make it happen, let everyone know about it. Put the exciting news in the brochure, on your website, as an announcement at the local schools, and in your press release.

Free Workshop

Schedule a free acting workshop for kids to try the class out. Let the parents attend as well.

During the workshop do the following:

- Welcome everyone to the free workshop.
- Play some drama games.
- Tell everyone why it is important for your organization to offer a drama program.
- Let the parents know the benefits for their children in taking a drama class.
- Play another game or two.
- Explain how your program works.
- If you are planning on having the kids perform for public access TV let the parents know all about it.

- Play one final game if you have the time and the kids are enthusiastic about it.
- Hand out literature and registration forms.
- You may want to offer a gift for the child (t-shirt, hat, duffle bag, toy, etc.) if the parent registers them before they leave.

You are on stage so be energetic. If you don't feel energetic, act energetic. After all, you are the drama teacher.

A PREP CLASS FOR THE SCHOOL PLAYS

Nearly every school puts on a play during the year.

Find out who the director of the school play is going to be and speak with them. Tell them about your drama program and "sell" the idea to the play director as a program that will prep the students for the play.

You may have to tweak a few things about your program to get the play director to buy into it. For example, she may want you to make sure they are prepared to project their voices. So this is something you would work more on during your classes.

 Once the director of the play is on board with your program and feels that it's something that can benefit her play (because what director doesn't want to work with actors who have taken acting classes?), ask her for a quote endorsing your program. Add the quote to your class description in the brochure and other marketing materials.

TALKING WITH OTHER AFTER SCHOOL CLASSES

You should be doing this already, but I know that marketing is not something we think about, running youth programs is.

Sometime during your other after school programs, especially when you have started registration for the following season, do a child friendly presentation about your new drama program.

Your presentation can be as simple as a quick speech or something more, like a skit that your staff performs.

You want to ensure that the kids know about the drama program and how fun it's going to be.

Then send them all home with a flyer to give to their parents.

KEEP A FILE OF ALL THE STUDENTS - EMAIL BLAST

At some point I learned how important it was to have relationships with parents.

I also learned the importance of having all the parents email addresses.

When this light bulb went off the organization I was working for didn't have on line registration and it was not common practice to gather email addresses of our customers.

So I started my own file.

Later in this chapter I will discuss the importance of emailing parents and how to get their email address if you don't already have it by way of registration.

With the file of names and email addresses that I had I would email all the parents of appropriate aged children about my new drama program. I would talk about the benefits, the format, and any other information I felt was pertinent.

This was also a good time to tell them about my free workshop that would introduce the program (if I was running one, of course).

This personal touch – yes, it is personal, much more so than a brochure you get in the mail – did wonders for my registrations.

 When you send out emails to parents take the time to type in their name on the email itself. Do not send out a general email that is sent to your list as "Dear Parent". Yes, sending them out one by one will take longer, but when a parent gets an email that is personal it makes all the difference. If you have an email program that does this automatically, your set.

Below is an example of how you should start an email that is promoting one of your programs or events.

Dear Barbara (or Mrs. Stephens, depending on your clientele),

> *I heard that Sarah is having a wonderful time in her scrapbooking class. She showed me what she's working on. She seems to really enjoy the class.*

> *I wanted to send you a quick note about a new drama program that I am offering in the fall. I think Sarah would have a great time. The reason we are running a drama program is because we believe in the benefits of a program like this. Those benefits being… (Write about the benefits and make sure the parents know that they can call*

you personally for more information.)

PHONE MESSAGE MACHINE

Use your out-of-office message and on-hold message to promote your program if possible.

Out-of-Office Message:

Hi this is Curt. I'm out of the office right now, but before you leave a message I want to make sure you are aware of an amazing new drama program that we are offering for middle school students.

Go to www.myorganization.com and click on the youth pages for more information. Have a great day. (beep)

On-Hold Message:

Confidence – Growth – Communication – Imagination. These are the traits and skills that young people get from a good drama program.

Even if your child has all these things they'll have a great time learning the basics of acting during our after school drama program.

Encore! is our drama class for 4th and 5th graders, while Young Actors Studio is for 6th and 7th graders.

Please log onto www.myorganization.com and click on the youth pages for more information.

PARTNER WITH SCHOOLS

These days schools seem be cutting their arts programs due to the lack of funding.

Drama always seems to be first on the chopping block.

It amazes me. I have used public speaking skills (going on interviews, leading staff trainings, pleading "not guilty" in traffic court, etc.) more than I have used algebra in my life, I suspect this is true for most adults. Yet drama is the first to go in a financial crunch.

While this is very unfortunate, it opens a door of opportunity for us.

Meet with the school principal or vice principal and see if you can help them out. Let them know that you are willing to offer a drama program for their students.

Your organization, of course, will take care of registration, but ask that the school offers all, or a combination of, the following;

- Space to run the after school program.
- Room on the bulletin board for a flyer to be posted.
- A blurb on their website.
- A chance to speak during the morning announcements.
- And anything else you can think of.

Partnerships with your local schools are crucial to your success.

 Get to know the secretaries and administrators. They can help you out like no other person or organization can.

ADVERTISE AT COMMUNITY EVENTS

Talk to people in the community and hand out information at local events.

Whether your organization, the Chamber of Commerce, the school, or another organization is putting on the event, ask if you can set up a table to promote your programs.

At the very least see if you can post information at their ticket booth or other prominent location.

HOLD A CONTEST AT SCHOOL

This is where your partnership with the schools can pay off.

Let the students, faculty, parents and anyone else you can think of, know about the contest you are holding.

Talent Show

Work with the school to organize a talent show during lunch time or on a specific evening.

Offer a trophy or some other prize for the winner.

You'll need to work with the school in creating a buzz about the event.

During the show have the MC promote your new drama program. Also, if possible have a banner made and displayed.

Best Skit

Run this the same way you would a talent show but instead of a variety of talents being showcased the students need to perform an original skit.

Karaoke

Who doesn't love to either perform or watch karaoke? Okay, so there are a few of you. There are a lot more of you who enjoy some good (or bad) singing.

Hold a karaoke contest and again, make sure you use it as a vehicle to promote your program.

Radio Theater

Have students create a 3-5 minute radio theater play, complete with sound effects.

Have them turn in their CD by a certain date.

Post all of them as podcasts on your website, or a dedicated podcast site.

Choose a winner or have other students vote for a winner.

During the podcasts or on the web page they are posted on, advertise your drama program.

Guessing Games

How many M&Ms are in the jar?

How many actors made over 1 million dollars last year?

How many actors and extras were in last night's episode of Hannah Montana?

Who will win the Oscars in the following categories?

Offer a couple of movie tickets for the winner(s) of whatever guessing game you decide to run.

When the kids come up to submit their guess give them a flyer for your program or at least talk about it.

When the winner is announced during the school announcements it should go something like this:

"Yesterday's M&M guessing contest is sponsored by (your organization). (Your

organization) is offering a fun and exciting drama program in the fall.

They'll make sure you're prepared for next year's school play. Get the edge by registering for the class today.

Now for the winner who will receive 2 movie tickets. The total number of M&Ms was 1254. With a guess of 1225 (student's name) is the winner. Congratulations, (student's name).

Please come to the office after school to claim your prize.

10 IDEAS FOR ONGOING MARKETING
OF YOUR DRAMA PROGRAM

Public Access T.V.

You may not know about your local public access television channel. Most of us have heard of public access but not too many people actually watch it.

If you tune to the public access channel you will see that there are various types of programming. During the day you will probably find that it is simply a community bulletin board that rotates announcements.

While I don't believe many people tune into public access programming there are definitely those who do. Posting on the community bulletin board is free.

- Call your local cable company and ask for the public access department, or
- Go online and search for your local public access station information
- Find out how you should submit your announcement. They will probably ask you to type your announcement up making sure you have contact information and then fax it into them. That's it. Free and easy.

I suggest you watch the community board to see how others format their announcements.

The second and more powerful medium you can use for your ongoing marketing efforts is on-air programming.

Public access stations are required to allow anyone who is a local resident to air programs on the channel. As long as you are not selling products and such you can air just about anything you want.

Public access stations are prohibited from controlling the content of the program that air. That means that you can air anything you want as long as it's not obscene.

The first thing you will need to do is contact the station and find out the procedures for submitting a program proposal.

You will most likely have to attend an orientation first. This orientation will inform you all about public access programming, the procedures for getting a program on the air and what the station offers.

Most public access stations offer all the equipment you need to put together a 30 minute or 1 hour program. From professional grade in-studio cameras, lighting, furniture, and audio equipment to all the field gear and editing equipment you may need to tape outside of the studio, they have it all.

Here's the best part, once you go through a couple of training classes they will let you use all their equipment for FREE! That's the beauty of public access.

So let's say you want to have your drama class do their performance in studio. You submit a program proposal. Once you get your times set up you take the kids into the studio and tape the program.

You will work out with the station when you want to see your program aired. Then you have the kids tell everyone they know that they are going to be on TV.

 Ask the schools to make an announcement with the time and channel of the program.

Imagine the buzz that you will create. Kids will be running to register for your next drama class.

T-SHIRTS AND POINTS

If you have handed out T-shirts to your students encourage the kids to wear them by offering them points each time they wear them to your class. You'll find that many of them will wear them all day at school before your class.

This is advertising for your program. Of course, some kids will put the shirt on right before they get to class, so be prepared for that and don't take it personally that they didn't wear the shirt all day.

So what are they trying to earn points for? Here are a few suggestions:

- End of session party
- A field trip to see a movie, go to dinner, or see a play.
- Prizes such as movie tickets, toys, DVD rentals, books, etc.

Many times I will give out points for behavior as well.

If you go with a points program make sure you keep an accurate total of each person's points. Also, be prepared to exclude those students who do not meet the point total.

Email the parents letting them know about the points program. Many parents will think it's a great idea and make sure their child is wearing the shirt.

If it's an end of session party or field trip that you are having the kids work towards, have them earn points as a group rather than individually. This ensures that they will keep each other in check and no one student will be excluded from the party or trip.

If the students do not get enough points do not let them have the reward. If the students fall short of the point goal and you give them a party anyways, the returning students will not take the points program seriously for the next session.

USE TESTIMONIALS

After your first session of classes has finished, email all of the parents and ask them to tell you what they thought of the program.

Be prepared for some constructive criticism. Constructive criticism is great. You can use the suggestions to make your program better. I love to get that kind of feedback.

The parents that email you back saying the program was great and their child enjoyed it should be contacted by email or phone and asked if they would allow you to use their comments in your brochure, website and other marketing materials.

It's always better to promote a program with testimonials like the one below.

"My child loved your drama program. She would come home after class and tell me all about the skits she was going to be in and the fun games she played. Thanks for a great program." Leslie Phillips

NEW SKETCHES

Many of the students you had for your first session will return for your next session since they enjoyed it so much.

Do not have them do the same sketches as last time. There may be a few that the kids love so much that you may want to bring them back, but for the most part you will want to make the second program completely different from the first.

Before your first session is over let the students know that you are offering the program again next season with a whole new set of sketches. They'll be excited about that.

You can find enough sketches (or skits) online to last you two to four sessions, but what about after that? What if you don't like the sketches that are out there?

My suggestion is to write your own.

Writing a 3-5 minute sketch is not that difficult when you use current events, movies, etc, as your inspiration.

Parodies of movies are always a great way to go. Parodies of popular commercials are good too. How about recreating a popular children's story like Hansel and Gretel or Goldilocks and the Three Bears?

Pull Your Bike Over!

In one community that I worked the police department was very serious about kids wearing helmets when riding their bicycles. The police were cracking down and they weren't being nice about it.

At the time I was working with middle school students and it was a big joke to them (though they always made sure they wore their helmets when they were riding). Even the parents thought it was ridiculous.

So I wrote a sketch that made fun of the whole thing. The parents and kids thought it was hilarious. It got a huge response and created a buzz at school the next day.

If you don't feel comfortable writing your own sketches ask a creative person you work with if they would collaborate with you.

When you get two or more people together to write a sketch, plan a new program, or plan an event the ideas seem to just flow. These brainstorming sessions usually end up being so much fun, many times they will go on for longer than you expected.

EMAIL PARENTS

We've talked about the different things you can do with email addresses and why they are so important to have.

The first thing you need to do is gather those email address.

When a parent registers their child for one of your programs call them and introduce yourself. Then ask them for their email address so that you can keep in touch with them regarding their child or any upcoming program or event that may be of interest to them.

Nearly all of the parents will view this as fantastic customer service.

REFER-A-FRIEND

You have probably heard of Refer-A-Friend programs. If not, the basic idea is that when someone refers a friend to sign up for one of your programs the person who referred them will get something for the referral, for example 10% or more off the next class they register for.

Give the kids an incentive in addition to, or instead of, the discount given to the parents. Examples might include a T-shirt, a hat, stuffed animal with your department logo, amusement park tickets, movie tickets, or a DVD.

YOUTUBE

Have someone video tape your performance.

Afterwards get written permission from all the parents of the students who were videotaped to put the videos on YouTube.

If they all give you permission then upload each sketch individually. I would then embed it onto your organizations website.

Make sure that all your students know that they are on YouTube so they can tell their friends.

INVITE EVERYONE

When you do your performance invite everyone you can including the mayor town council, the School board, the P.T.A., the local newspaper, etc. The more exposure you get the better your chances to grow the program.

Having the local newspaper come and take pictures will work wonders. Having them there will be better than your own press release.

PERFORM IN PUBLIC

This is fun. During a community event have your drama team perform for an audience.

Choose your best sketch.

Make sure all the students can make it. Trust me they will love the opportunity to perform for others.

This shows the community that you and your organization are offering wonderful youth programs that the kids are enjoying. The community may suspect that you are running quality programs, but this really brings it to life.

OPEN HOUSE

Hold an open house for all of your programs.

Set up arts and crafts projects that the kids have made, sports demonstrations, student performances, enlarged pictures or posters of the participants, etc. Have all of the staff there to answer questions, take registrations, and help with all the details of set up, clean up and running the event.

For the drama program have your class perform or show a video of the classes and performance, post pictures and have literature out.

Attend the local schools' Open Houses. Ask the principals of the local elementary and middle schools if you can attend them in order to inform the parents of the wonderful after school programs you offer their students.

7

THE FINAL ACT

10 TIPS AND TRICKS WORTH KNOWING ABOUT

In this chapter I have included 10 tips and tricks that either didn't fit into any other section of this book or I wanted to reiterate because I felt it was important.

PUBLIC ACCESS T.V.

Earlier, I discussed the wonderful world of public access television. This is a powerful marketing tool.

First, you entice kids and parents into registering with the allure of being on TV. How exciting!

Second, the students who are on TV will be the ones telling all their friends and classmates that they are going to be on TV. The more who watch the program the better it will be.

I want to go over exactly how to get your drama program – or any other program – on public access television.

Provided you are not selling or marketing a product or service, you can produce and air your very own television show for free. The use of studio, field and editing equipment will not cost you a dime. The staff you need for your production will volunteer their time. This incredible opportunity exists nearly everywhere in the U.S.

Your Local Cable Company

Contact your local cable company and ask them to connect you to the public access department.

You can also go online and search for your city, cable company, and "public access". They may have all the information you need at their website.

The steps below may vary depending on the guidelines of your local cable company. I will go through the steps that I am accustomed to.

The Orientation

Register to attend an orientation. This is a free class and anyone who wants to do anything on public access must go through this step.

Depending on your local station they may offer the orientation once a month or even once every six months. So sign up now, because this may take a while.

The Studio Class

Next you will need to register for the studio class where you will be taught the basics of how to run the in-studio equipment. This is usually a one-day class. Once you have completed it you can have the station add your name to the volunteer list for future productions.

Your Program

Come up with a program idea and write a draft of the script. Shows on public access are either 30 minutes or one hour.

Politics, religion, cooking, entertainment, history, parenting, children's, and how-to programming are all examples of what is aired on public access.

Field Equipment

If you need to record outside of the studio you'll need to submit your proposal and then register for the Field Equipment Class.

Program Proposal

Now you'll need to fill out a Program Proposal.

Public access stations have no editorial control over the programming. Generally, the only guidelines are that it must be non-commercial and follow FCC regulations (i.e. no nudity, obscenity, etc.).

Studio Time

Once your program proposal is accepted (which really depends on air time and not much else) studio time will be assigned for you and your crew. The station will probably give you 1 evening of studio time for a 30 min. show and 2 evenings for an hour show.

Your Crew

Gather your crew. Most of us don't have 8 people who will go through the training with us.

Thankfully, the stations have lists of people who have taken the classes and would love to volunteer, either for the experience or for fun. Get a copy of the list and start calling.

Lights, Camera, Action

On the evening of the taping it is always nice to feed your crew. It's not mandatory, but volunteers appreciate having some sandwiches or pizza and beverages available.

Once the lighting is set and your on-camera talent (which may be you) is ready then it's time to start.

The Director

One of your volunteers will be the director whose name you will have gotten off the director list. This person will have experience with all the facets of programming. Use their knowledge and experience.

This is your show so don't be shy letting the director know exactly what you want, but give them some freedom to make it happen.

After a few shows you will get the hang of how everything happens and, unless you are the on-air talent, will then want to direct it all yourself.

Your Show Airs

Public Access doesn't advertise their shows, so if you want anyone to see it then you'll need to get the word out. Start with family, friends and co-workers.

POP CULTURE AND SKETCH WRITING

Writing sketches/skits is not that difficult when you use pop culture as your inspiration. Take a cartoon, TV show, commercial or movie that the kids enjoy or talk about a lot and make a spoof of it. Ask yourself "What If?"

Here are some "What Ifs" to get you started

1. What if Sponge Bob Square Pants had a sister or family?

2. What if Hannah Montana was 65 years old?

3. What if Survivor was in South Central L.A.?

4. What if a TV producer decided to do a show called the Biggest Gainer instead of the Biggest Loser and all the contestants put on as much weight as they could?

5. What if Harry Potter became a school janitor, or a cop, or a baseball player?

6. What if one of Harry Potter's kids turned out to be a Muggle?

7. What if Mickey Mouse was a teacher at the school?

8. What if the kids played superheroes when they were young and at school. How would Superman, Aquaman, Wonder Woman, and Spider-

man have acted as 6th graders?

 Make sure you keep the intended audience in mind when you write your scripts. Sure, some parents might know about the R.U.F.F. cartoon series, but not many of them will. Most parents, however, will have seen at least a few episodes of Sponge Bob.

CRAIGSLIST AND THRIFT SHOPS

If you're lucky enough to be in an area that has Craigslist check it often for the props you need.

Also check the "free stuff" regularly. A lot of people don't want to go through the hassle of selling their items, but they don't want to just throw them away either.

Craigslist is a wonderful resource for all kinds of items. It's a 24/7 garage sale.

You can also place a free ad asking for props that you need.

Thrift shops are another great resource. Visit the local thrift shops with your prop list in hand. You never know what you're going to find.

ASK THE STUDENTS

Speaking of props, one of the things I do every class is give a list of props I need and ask the students to take it home and see if they have the items or if their parents can help.

Anytime you do not need to spend money on props you obviously keep your expenses down. Of course, I have built up a nice collection of costumes and various props that I had to buy at one time or another.

If you have to purchase items make sure you keep them in an assigned area. You may not use them during your next class but you'll be glad you kept them for the following one.

SURVEYS

After my program ends I send an email to all the parents that has a link to a survey. I want to know what they thought of the class and how I might be able to improve.

This also gives me a chance to test out any new program ideas I might have.

Here is a sample of a 10-question survey I would send out.

1. Did your child enjoy the drama class? If not, why?
2. Has your child ever taken a drama class before?
3. Has your child ever participated in any of our other programs? If yes, which ones?
4. How was the instructor?
5. Did you enjoy the performance?
6. If we offered a drama program again would your child be interested in attending?
7. Are there any suggestions you have for improving the program?
8. During the fall we are considering offering a Hip Hop Dance class. Is this something your child would be interested in?
9. We have also considered putting together a family friendly haunted house for Halloween. Is this something your family would attend?
10. Do you have any suggestions for other after school programs or special events we should be running?

Thank you for your participation in this short 10-question survey. The instructor was thrilled to have such a wonderful group of kids to teach.

As you can see I have used surveys to feel out what people think of other ideas I may have for future programs and events. It also shows that you are interested in what the community thinks.

Of course, in order to send out surveys you will need to have the parents email addresses. Get this either when they register or call them and get it after the class has started.

There are plenty of online survey companies that you can use. Some of them will let you use their limited services for free.

Survey Monkey

Survey Monkey is the online survey company that I use. Their service is free as long as you don't need to create surveys of more than 10 questions. I find that if surveys are much longer than 10 questions many people won't participate in them anyways.

Survey Monkey is also easy to use. You create a survey using one of their templates and send the link to your email list with a little note asking the parents to please participate in a short 10 question survey.

Survey Monkey also has extra services that you can pay for.

DISNEY USES LOTS OF COLOR

Do you ever watch the Disney Channel? Have you ever been to Disneyland or Disney World? They make the most of color.

If you watch a Disney show you'll see that the actors wear very colorful clothes, the walls are painted various colors, etc.

Use color.

If you can have your props various colors then do so. If you can get costumes that are colorful, do it.

Have your students wear different colors. Have them stay away from grey, black, brown, etc. Colors are pleasing to the eye.

It's a little thing that makes a big difference.

KEEP YOUR SANITY - FIND HELP FOR THE PERFORMANCE

You have successfully run a drama program for ten weeks all by yourself. No problem.

Though you can run the performance on your own I highly suggest you enlist the help of two other staff. I speak from experience.

From opening and closing the curtain to getting the props ready and keeping the students under control, you will have so many other things to think about that you will need and appreciate the help.

THE LIBRARY IS YOUR FRIEND

Use your local library for books that I recommend in the Resources section. Log onto your library's website and check to see if your library or one of its sister libraries carry them.

 Generally if your local library doesn't carry a particular book but one of the other libraries do then you can request it be sent to your local library for a nominal charge. My library charges $0.50. It's a lot cheaper and more convenient than driving to the other library to get the book.

GOOGLE BOOK SEARCH

Google Book Search is another great tool that you should be aware of. I use it for two things.

1. A lot of books that you may be searching for have previews. Google has

scanned pages of the book for you to look at.

If the book does have a preview then you will be able to read the table of contents as well as the first couple of chapters and perhaps more.

This is useful when you want to check out a book that you are interested in purchasing. It beats Amazon's "Look Inside" feature.

2. It will show you the nearest library that is carrying the book you are looking for.

    This is very helpful if your local library system does not carry the book you want but you are willing to go to another town that is near, as opposed to purchasing the book.

Say Cheese!

Parents love to see their kids having fun and learning at the same time.

During your classes take pictures of the students participating in the theater games and rehearsing their sketches.

There are three things you can do with those pictures:

1. Post them on a specific page of your organizations website.

    Password protect that particular page if you are concerned about parents getting upset. I haven't seen this as a problem before, but you never know.

    You can always ask the parents if it would be okay to post pictures of their children on your site. This is probably the best way to go.

2. Email them right to the parents with a little note about how the classes are going.

3. If you want to go all out, get some inexpensive frames and choose a picture or two for each student.

    Present them to the students or their parents to take home after the performance.

RESOURCES

BOOKS AND SITES THAT ARE WORTH THE LOOK

I have listed the books and websites that have helped me create a successful drama program. Check for any of the books on Amazon and you will see a few more publications that may interest you.

BOOKS

101 Improv Games, by Bob Bedore
A wonderful book of improv games for children and adults of all experience levels. I have a couple of other improv books but this is the one I always use.

Theater Games for Young Performers, by Maria C. Novelly
This book is specifically geared towards youth and includes games, exercises, worksheets and more. I don't use the worksheets but I use a number of the activities from the book.

On Stage: Theater Games and Activities for Kids, by Lisa Bany-Winters
This book is written for young actors between 1st and 6th grade. It includes classic drama games and activities, mask making, costuming, some set design and several short scripts. I like the way this book is put together. The scripts aren't that great in my opinion but the rest of the book is. Keep in mind though that this book is written for kids. You'll find it in the juvenile section of your local library.

Kids Take the Stage: Helping Young People Discover the Creative Outlet of Theater, by Lenka Peterson
This is a neat book for teachers. It shows how to get a production up and running. By production I mean a play not a series of sketches. This book is not necessarily an easy read but there is a lot of good information in it. It's the first book I bought when I created my drama program.

The Skit Book: 101 Skits From Kids, by Margaret Read MacDonald
This book is full of short easy skits for kids. I like to take some of these skits and expand them into a more robust sketch. It's a great reference.

Break a Leg: The Kids Guide to Acting and Stagecraft, by Lise Friedman
If you want to take your class to a full program this is a great book to get. It includes tips on warming up, stage combat, musical theater, character building, analyzing a script, encores, costuming, headshots and much more. It's a wonderful book to have in your collection.

WEBSITES

Recreation Pros
To download the sketches/skits that I use for my classes go to visit:
http://recreationpros.com/skit_book

Ultimate Camp Resource
Anybody can contribute to their growing collection of games and other information. The part you would be interested in is the section on skits.
http://www.ultimatecampresource.com

Scout-O-Rama
Here is another collection of skits. These are posted mostly by scouts so many of them aren't exactly well written on the site. However, you can find a lot of skits here.
http://www.scoutorama.com/skit

Improv Encyclopedia
If you are looking for more theater improv games this is the site. It has an extensive list of theater games that are described in detail.
http://www.improvencyclopedia.org

Made in the USA
Lexington, KY
10 November 2014